Original title:
Ferns in the Window

Copyright © 2025 Creative Arts Management OÜ
All rights reserved.

Author: Maxwell Donovan
ISBN HARDBACK: 978-1-80581-822-9
ISBN PAPERBACK: 978-1-80581-349-1
ISBN EBOOK: 978-1-80581-822-9

Whispering Leaves and Morning Sun

In the morning light they sway,
Little green dancers start to play.
Whispering secrets to the breeze,
While sipping sunshine with such ease.

Tickling dust with gentle grace,
They take the sun's warm, smiling face.
Plotting mischief from their spot,
A leafy coup that can't be caught.

Captive Growths of the Urban Heart

Stuck in pots but feeling grand,
Dream of jungles, bright and planned.
With roots in soil, they laugh and stretch,
Urban life, their charm bewitched.

Watching humans rush around,
While they lounge without a sound.
Oh, what a show when leaves turn bright,
A green parade in morning light.

The Quiet Presence of Green

Quiet whispers fill the room,
Overtaking all the gloom.
With leafy hands they wave hello,
To passersby, their charming show.

Never asking much at all,
Just a sip when shadows fall.
In their stillness, smiles are found,
A private joke, lightly wound.

Fragrant Odes to Indoor Life

In pots they seed their witty lore,
With stories told of days of yore.
The air gets filled with hints of fun,
As they dance beneath the sun.

Green jesters living side by side,
With every breeze, they take a ride.
Who knew that life could be so sweet,
With leafy friends at our retreat?

An Oasis of Green Dreams

Little leaves waving high,
Reaching for the ceiling sky,
Whispers of a leafy joke,
In the pot, a green cloak.

Dust bunnies flee in fright,
As leaves dance with delight,
A tiny bug hops by,
Winking with a sly eye.

Enchanted Leaves of the Indoors

A sprig so sprightly sways,
Picking up the light's rays,
Joking with the windowpane,
Free from worrying rain.

Laughter fills the air,
As plants sway without care,
With a twist, and a curl,
It's a leafy carousel.

Lush Echoes of Home

In the corner, a tribe of green,
Exchanging tales, quite serene,
With a grin, they softly sigh,
And dream of the sunlit sky.

Nature's jesters claim the space,
Spreading joy with leafy grace,
While we ponder, lost in thought,
Do they know what we've sought?

A Tapestry of Green Life

Woven strands of vibrant hue,
Telling stories, old and new,
Rooted jokes from deep below,
Giggling as they start to grow.

Reaching for a sip of sun,
These little gremlins have their fun,
In the quietness they play,
Turning mundane into ballet.

A Verdant Interlude of Growing Life

I found a plant that waves hello,
With leaves that dance and put on a show.
It mimics me, in quirky styles,
And makes me laugh for quite a while.

In morning light, it beams with glee,
A leafy creature, wild and free.
With tiny pots, its pals abound,
Together, they do twirl around.

Fronds of Comfort in Close Quarters

In crowded rooms, they spread their arms,
With leafy charms and subtle balms.
They whisper jokes in playful tones,
And thrive on silliness, like clones.

Gathered round, they share the space,
No elbow room, but plenty of grace.
They snicker softly, green and proud,
In every corner, they stand loud.

Lush Green Echoes of Nature Indoors

From shelves and nooks, they peek with joy,
Each leaf a look, each frond a ploy.
In silent chuckles, they seem to share,
The quirks of living, the joy of care.

They hear my jokes, and giggle low,
A leafy audience, putting on a show.
They stretch and nod, with lighthearted glee,
Nature's laughter, so wild and free.

Guardians of the Warm Rays

These green companions bask in light,
Filching warmth from day to night.
They guard the beams like little spies,
With goofy grins and watchful eyes.

When I forget to water, they pout,
With droopy heads, they often doubt.
But once I sprinkle them with care,
They bounce back up, beyond compare.

Fronds of Hope in Urban Shadows

With leafy arms stretched out wide,
They dance with every passing breeze,
In concrete jungles, they abide,
Making homes in glassy seas.

A quirky sight above the street,
They wink at pigeons strutting by,
While taxi drivers tap their feet,
A riot of green, oh my, oh my!

Tiny critters sneak a peek,
As sunbeams spill their gold in streams,
With every week, they seem to speak,
Of urban myths and leafy dreams.

In pots with soil that's somewhat shy,
They giggle at the busy throngs,
In plastic homes, they flutter high,
With whispers soft, they sing their songs.

Bittersweet Symphony of Green

In windowpanes, they catch the light,
Frolicking midst the bustling days,
A symphony of green delight,
Playing tricks in playful ways.

They peek at lunch from plates nearby,
A little dance on porcelain's edge,
With laughter soft, they slyly lie,
While crumbs tumble like a hedge.

In laughter's echo, twirls abound,
Each frond a jester in its right,
They sway to city's humming sound,
In leafy gowns, alive with fright.

The sunlight glows like giggling friends,
As shadows stretch and skip around,
To watch them sway is bliss that bends,
As life's odd melody is found.

Through Transparent Veils of Nature

Curly greens with a secret laugh,
They stick their tongues out at the rain,
Through glassy walls, they tell their half,
Of tales where sunlight flew the lane.

Casting shadows in an artful haze,
They wiggle whimsically, it seems,
With every drizzle, they amaze,
As sprightly dancers in our dreams.

A curious leaf peeks at the cat,
Who watches back with half at ease,
A silent truce where all is fat,
With giggles echoing on the breeze.

In sill life's quirky little game,
With playful hearts that twine and spin,
Each frond has its own little fame,
In nature's sketch, we all dive in.

Wildlings Within Embraced Spaces

Chasing sunlight from their cozy spots,
These wildlings play as if they'd won,
With smiles strung on weathered pots,
They twirl and leap, oh what a fun!

Invisible friends in green attire,
Who speak in rustles, soft and bright,
They stir the air with leafy fire,
Drawn to every splash of light.

As window whispers weave through time,
They plot adventures by the moon,
With thoughts so wild, and oh so prime,
Their joy erupts like springtime's tune.

In every nook, they make their claim,
With hugs of growth and playful cheer,
In shared spaces, they stake their fame,
From city streets to skies so clear.

The Indoor Canopy

Up high they dance, a leafy crew,
Whispering tales, oh, what a view!
Each frond conspires, plotting all day,
To steal your snacks, in their own leafy way.

With sunlight beams, they stretch and sway,
Hiding from cats, who dare to play.
In battles of dust, they brush and tease,
Claiming the sun, as if they please.

Serene Reflections in the Quiet Room

In corners they plot with a tranquil air,
Mimicking yoga poses, unaware.
A zen-like calm, they bide their time,
While plotting to sneak snacks, in rhythm and rhyme.

They giggle at the shadows on the wall,
Pretending they're dancers, in concert hall.
With every breeze, a soft little sway,
Who knew houseplants could have such a play?

Choreography of Chlorophyll

With a twist and a turn, they show their groove,
Those green little dancers, in their leafy move.
Weaving through sunlight, they're a lively crew,
All in sync, with a fresh morning dew.

As the cat takes a leap, they playfully duck,
In this lively waltz, no room for bad luck.
Laughing at gravity, they leap and glide,
A botanical ballet, with nowhere to hide.

Embracing the Leafy Glow

In the warm glow, they soak up the light,
Basking in fame, they're feeling quite bright.
Sharing secrets with dust, oh what a sight,
As they plot their mischief, just out of sight.

Each leaf a comedian, in life's quick show,
Ninja-like stealth, as they rustle and grow.
With a sip of water, they laugh and sing,
In their leafy wonderland, they're the green king.

Flourishing Vignettes of Interior Nature

In pots where green things thrive,
A dance of shadows comes alive.
Leaves whisper secrets, soft with glee,
"Who knew we'd host such a jubilee?"

Mossy hats on each frond sway,
Inviting cats to join the play.
Birds outside just scoff and laugh,
"Those plants sure know how to have a laugh!"

Sunbeams bounce on emerald scales,
As laughter floats on gentle gales.
A kaleidoscope of leaf and vine,
Each one claims a little shrine.

Friends of soil and happy air,
We gleam with joy and little care.
In this little world so bright,
We're the jesters, pure delight!

The Allure of Indoor Greenwaves

In the sunny nook, leaves twirl,
Like tiny dancers in a whirl.
They wave hello with gentle flair,
"Come join us, don't you dare not care!"

The cat thinks them a jungle gym,
To perch upon the leafy rim.
Yet bumping little colas rise,
"Not too wild! We're not a prize!"

A playful breeze brings whispers near,
Of tiny tales that find an ear.
What's that? A leaf's giggle here,
"Oops! I dropped a dew! Come leer!"

Windows glow with leafy cheer,
The world's outside just disappears.
A kingdom of green, what a scene,
In our quirky, leafy routine!

Shoals of Green Treasures

A flotilla of greens afloat,
Like submarines in sunbeam coat.
"Arr matey," they seem to say,
"Join us for adventure today!"

In each pot, a pirate's dream,
Swashbuckling in a leafy stream.
Rummaging through soil, they seek,
Treasure hidden at the peak.

Ye dandy fronds, all spruced up,
Convene around a drinking cup.
Quench your thirst, oh merry guise,
A sip of sunlight, sweet surprise!

Each leaf a giggle, green and spry,
They chuckle softly, way up high.
Home of mischief, made to please,
A playful corner, nature's tease!

Bounty of the Leafy Abode

In the corner, plants conspire,
To be the chatty guest of fire.
"Don't fret the weeding or the dust,
We're here for laughter, that's a must!"

Each curl and twist, a story told,
Of sunny days and leafy gold.
"We dream of butterflies and bees,
And sip on raindrops with the trees!"

The pot grows wise with every sun,
"Frolic on, my little ones!"
Curious critters peek and stare,
"Is there a party? We want flair!"

Green guardians of indoor mirth,
Spreading joy across the earth.
In our little haven, oh, so wide,
The bounty laughs, let's bide our tide!

Living Elegance in Unadorned Spaces

In corners where the dust bunnies play,
A leafy friend begins its ballet.
It sways to the tunes of a breezy beat,
Waving its fronds, oh what a feat!

With no fancy pots or grand designs,
Just sunlight and love, it brightly shines.
A subtle dance, no spotlight to steal,
Just charming whispers, oh what a deal!

It doesn't ask for much, just a sip,
A drink of water, a little trip.
To the sink for a rinse, then back to its nook,
Living things need love, just like a good book!

So let's raise a glass to its leafy parade,
A silent performer in its grand charade.
In spaces quite plain, it finds its stance,
The understated diva, alive in a dance!

Softly Unfurled in Morning Warmth

As sunlight creeps across the floor,
Bright green fingers stretch and explore.
They wave hello to sleepy souls,
In morning light, they play their roles.

No need for coffee or fancy toast,
These leafy beings are what we boast.
With gentle curls, they tease the day,
In the kitchen corner, they come out to play!

A flicker of shadow, a rustle of cheer,
Each little frond knows no fear.
They sway to the comedy of life's own plot,
In their leafy embrace, we forget what we've got.

So laugh with the leaves, let your worries take flight,
In their playful presence, the world feels right.
For in their simple green, we find delight,
Softly unfurling, morning's own sight!

A Refuge of Leafy Serenity

In a quiet nook where mischief waddles,
Leaves laugh quietly, playing in squads.
They whisper secrets of days gone past,
In green-hued wonder, the moments last.

A hideaway where chaos won't dwell,
Among the leaves, all stories swell.
Here's a fine spot to rest your thoughts,
With leafy limbs that tie up knots.

They hide from the drama of daily hustle,
With nature's grace, they create a bustle.
No need for drama, just a soft sigh,
In their leafy embrace, let the world fly by.

So take a seat and breathe in deep,
Let leafy guardians put you to sleep.
In this refuge—oh so serene,
Life's little follies become routine!

Nature's Guardians of Solitude

In a world that spins with frantic pace,
These quiet greens find their place.
They guard our secrets, our soft-spoken dreams,
In leafy laughter, nothing is as it seems.

With fronds held high and shadows nearby,
They're the jesters, watch them fly!
They giggle at worries we dare to share,
In their leafy realm, there's freedom in air.

When the world feels heavy, and life feels tough,
These guardians whisper, 'Hey, it's enough!'
They'll huddle close, with no need for a roar,
In soft solitude, find joy at your door.

So tip your hat to the green brigade,
They'll keep you smiling, never afraid.
In their leafy embrace, take a wild ride,
Nature's guardians, forever our guide!

Fronds Embracing the Glass

Green fingers wave, oh what a sight,
Dance with the dust, in soft sunlight.
They tilt and they twirl, a leafy parade,
Unaware of the games that sunlight has played.

A wiggle and shuffle, they start to conspire,
Telling the world they're a little bit higher.
With sarcasm stitched in each gentle line,
They giggle at pots, 'We're stylish, divine!'

Life Behind Crystal Barriers

Is it a jungle or garden attire?
Behind the glass, they conspire and wire.
Plotting mischief in the midday glare,
With leafy whispers, 'Who's going out there?'

Each sip of sunshine, they gulp and they bloat,
'Keep the curtains closed!' they all seem to gloat.
With roots in the pot, they're kings of the climb,
Painting their antics in chlorophyll rhyme.

Shadows of Ferns in Sunlight

Sunbeams tickle, casting shadows so spry,
Frolicking ferns, waving to the sky.
'Look at us dance!' says the one on the sill,
As a gnat takes a tumble, oh what a thrill!

The ghost of a leaf flits past like a dream,
Lurking and laughing, it's all in the scheme.
'Catch us if you can!' they snicker and tease,
In a whimsical waltz with the soft summer breeze.

Nature's Embrace at Home

In cozy corners, they like to reside,
Crack jokes with the sunlight, they won't ever hide.
Spreading their arms in a quirky embrace,
Sprinkled with laughter, they brighten the place.

A smirk on the stem, a giggle in green,
'This home is a stage, and we reign as the queen!'
They know that the windows can make for a show,
With each playful wave, they steal the whole glow.

Fern Kingdoms in the Sun's Embrace

In the corner, big leaves prance,
Dancing wildly, oh what a chance!
They sway with joy, a leafy show,
Pretending they're in a jungle, you know.

Little pots with secrets deep,
Whispering tales while we sleep.
They nod and wink, as if to say,
"Join us in our leafy play!"

A crown of green, a royal sight,
Living castles, just out of sight.
They plot their journey to the floor,
To escape the rays and dance some more.

With sunlight spilling through the glass,
They hold court, letting time pass.
In their reign, they spread such cheer,
Oh, how they thrive, year after year!

Life's Breath in Sheltered Corners

In cozy nooks where shadows loom,
Leaves shake off the dust of gloom.
With every breeze, a gentle tease,
Who knew green could giggle with ease?

They plot adventures with each curl,
Chasing dust bunnies, oh what a swirl!
They nod their heads, and we can't help,
But chuckle at their leafy yelp.

In high sun, they stretch and flare,
Making sunlight a circus affair.
With leafy friends, they laugh and twine,
Creating jokes in the sunshine.

Oh, how they thrive, seekers of fun,
Turning chores into games, just begun.
In every petal, a secret told,
About laughter and joy that never gets old.

Windowsill Verdure and Dappled Light

On windowsills where laughter grows,
Tiny trees in tidy rows.
They peek at passersby outside,
With thumbs up, they share their pride.

A bit too close to sizzling rays,
Yet they thrive on sunny days.
With twists and turns, they play the game,
Gossiping leaves, who's to blame?

In the dance of shadows, they smile bright,
Flaunting their green in the soft twilight.
With every inch, they corkscrew tight,
Daring the world to share their plight.

Oh, these plants, such quirky bunch,
Making every meal a Sunday brunch.
In dappled light, they live the dream,
While plotting for the next leafy scheme.

Green Embrace of Urban Life

Amidst the concrete and rushing feet,
Lies a green kingdom, oh what a feat!
With roots that giggle at city strife,
Creating their joy in city life.

They peek from ledges with leafy grins,
Ready for laughter, ready to win.
A whiff of fun with a splash of green,
Turning busy days into a delightful scene.

In the sun's glow, they stretch and puff,
Ready to share all their leafy stuff.
"Come join the party, leave your care!"
In their green arms, there's always a chair.

So here's to joy, in every frond,
A playful twist of life to respond.
In urban chaos, they find their way,
Bringing chuckles to every day.

Nature's Artistry Behind Pane

On the sill, they lean with flair,
Dancing shadows, quite the pair.
Whispers of green, with a cheeky grin,
Sway to the rhythm, where to begin?

Neighbors peek in, with eyes so wide,
What magic concocts this leafy ride?
An indoor jungle, but with no wild beast,
Just playful greens having a feast!

Tiny hands waving from each lush tip,
Invitation to join in their quirky trip.
They giggle and giggle, oh what a sight,
Turning my gloom into sheer delight!

Nature's brush strokes, scattered with glee,
Art behind glass, as vibrant as can be.
With each sunbeam, they twirl and spin,
Life's fun little rascals, let the game begin!

Solace in Emerald Hues

Sitting quiet, they bask in cheer,
Whispering secrets for me to hear.
With emerald cloaks, they seem to say,
'Join our fun, let worries stray!'

A humble patch of nature's delight,
Painting the room in shades so bright.
Their leaves remind me of green jelly,
Wobbling softly, oh so smelly!

Each leaf's a goofy grin just for me,
Laughing and playing, so carefree.
In my room, they plot and scheme,
Cooking up adventures like ice cream!

With a sprinkle of sunlight, they come alive,
Joking and jiggling as they thrive.
A testament to laughter, oh so true,
In shades of green, they sing 'Woo-hoo!'

The Gentle Guardians of Light

Guardians of light, they stand so tall,
Waving softly, they beckon all.
With every beam, a wily wink,
'Come sit with us, have a drink!'

They catch the sun in a playful trap,
Glimmers of joy in a leafy lap.
A green team ready for mischief to hatch,
Each frond a plan, each leaf a catch!

Peering out, they spot the world,
Watching life swirl and twirl,
'Look, a squirrel! Oh what a sight!'
They giggle at creatures, oh what a fright!

Stealthy spies of the nature's show,
In a leafy robes, they steal the glow.
So lighthearted, with a twist of fate,
Their antics are written, oh so great!

Fronded Thoughts in Breezy Stillness

In a world of whispers, they softly muse,
Fronded thoughts drift, as the light renews.
With a jiggle and shake, they tell their tales,
Of sunlight dances and stormy gales.

Huddled close, they plot their schemes,
Mixing up trouble in leafy dreams.
'What if we wave when the dog walks by?'
Their giggles erupt as they reach for the sky!

They sway with the breeze, a synchronized crew,
Spin and twirl like they have something to prove.
A frothy green café where fun likes to meet,
Sipping on sunshine—it's quite the treat!

With nature's flair, they chaotically blend,
Every tilt and turn is a curveball send.
In my window, their laughter resounds,
Echoing joy in these leafy bounds!

Embracing the Gentle Caress of Green

In corners they plot, oh what a design,
Hiding from dust, they sip on sunshine.
With leaves that wave like they're at a ball,
Whispering secrets, they're having a ball.

Each day they grow a little more bold,
Telling the stories that never get old.
They chuckle at cats who can't reach the shelf,
Making the world feel like a joyful elf.

They're sprouting their dreams, oh how they thrive,
In pots that make them feel quite alive.
Messy with soil, they don't seem to care,
A ruckus of green in the cozy air.

With every new leaf, a giggle is shared,
While webs of dust grow, they never get scared.
A party of greens does a dance in the light,
Who knew houseplants could be such a sight?

The Solace of Soft Green Shadows

In the window they lounge, with elegance supreme,
   Casting soft shadows, how it makes me beam.
    A leafy ballet, in the bright afternoon,
They twirl and they twist to the song of the moon.

    Each petal adorned with a cheeky grin,
    Teasing the sunlight to let the fun in.
  And when I walk by, they muster a cheer,
   A comedy troupe in a vibrant frontier.

They gossip with dust on a lazy afternoon,
 Plotting their routes to the nearest good spoon.
"More water!" they shout though they're hardly dry,
   With antics so wild, I can't help but sigh.

They seem to conspire, in green jesters garb,
   Waving goodbye to my feeble drab.
Who knew ferns could be the life of the show?
In their leafy embrace, I'm never feeling low.

Echoes of Ancient Forests in Glass

In a pot by the sill, they channel the past,
Dancing to echoes that forever last.
Roots tangled like stories, leaves waving with glee,
Whispering wisdom just for me.

They argue with sunlight about who shines best,
Declaring it's them, while I just jest.
A tangle of laughs, shenanigans bright,
In the realm of the glass, they're pure delight.

With each little frond, they can't help but tease,
Swapping old tales with the soft summer breeze.
They thrive on my jokes, a whimsical crowd,
Guardians of giggles, they stand so proud.

Ancient companions, full of tales they bring,
Echoing laughter, life's fruitful fling.
Who knew being green could be such a hoot?
In this glassy dominion, they take root.

Silhouettes of Life Beyond Glass

In muted light, they stretch and they play,
Shadows on walls take me far away.
Each leaf a character, each stem a scene,
In this drama of green, I'm forever keen.

Their stories unfold with a flick of a tip,
As I sip my tea in this leafy trip.
A bunch of green pals, they laugh at my plight,
Twirling in whispers of a starry night.

They thumb their noses at the rain on the street,
While I make new plans for a festival treat.
With every new sprout, they join in the fun,
Who knew being green could outshine the sun?

So here in this home, they quietly conspire,
With shadows and giggles, they never tire.
While I watch in awe, they put on a show,
Silhouettes of joy in the light's gentle glow.

Curves of Life Beneath the Glass

In a pot on the sill, they sway and twist,
A jungle of greens, they can't be missed.
They're plotting a dance, oh what a sight,
  Mossy little rebels, feeling just right.

The sunlight beams, a spotlight cheer,
They wiggle their leaves, they're shedding fear.
A leaf drops down like a wayward joke,
  "Oops, sorry folks, I just lost my cloak!"

With soil pals nearby, they share their dreams,
  Imagining walks on shimmering streams.
  Sipping on water, they raise a toast,
  "Here's to the rays! We're the leafy most!"

So if you peek in, just give a grin,
  These little green stars are ready to win.
With laughter and cheer, they'll take their bow,
  "Behold our performance! We're epic now!"

Indoor Wilderness

In the corner of curiosity and flair,
A playful bunch stretching without a care.
They whisper of jungles, of faraway lands,
With taciturn secrets and leafy hands.

A visitor comes with a puzzled look,
"Is this a plant or a storybook?"
They giggle in silence, their humor wild,
"Just mind your manners, you charming child!"

With spritz of water, they stand up straight,
"Another sip!" they cry, "It's never too late!"
To waltz in the breeze, they playfully vow,
"Indoor adventurers, we're taking a bow!"

So glance at the greenery, that much is true,
In this wild kingdom, they're waiting for you.
With laughter and life, they twirl and they sway,
"Join our shenanigans, come out and play!"

The Repose of Leafy Dreams

Nestled within a glassy embrace,
They lounge with style in their cozy place.
Dreaming of forests, they take it slow,
"Another five minutes, just let us glow!"

With whimsical patterns, they wiggle and bend,
"Who needs a breeze? We've got our friends!"
A tumble of soil, a mischievous sprout,
"Oops, my bad! Let's all dance about!"

They pad through the sunlight, gentle and bright,
"More of that warmth, it feels so right!"
With a puff of their leaves, they share a laugh,
"Living the dream, we're not just a half!"

So come take a peek at their leafy delight,
These jokesters of green stir up pure light.
In their lazy repose, they'll always reprise,
"Join our leafy laughter, it's quite the surprise!"

Airy Elegance on Display

In the window's embrace, they swish and sway,
With elegance bold, they steal the day.
"Look at us shine!" they chatter in green,
"A garden of giggles, just look at the scene!"

They prance in their pots, a charming ballet,
"Who needs a stage? We're fun in our way!"
A leaf fancies itself quite the grand star,
"Watch me, don't blink, I'm raising the bar!"

A friend peeks in, the laughter roars,
"Do you come from the wild? We're never outdoors!"
With whispers how sweet, their spirits ignite,
"Join our leafy frolic, it's pure delight!"

As shadows grow long and the sun bows low,
They wave their green arms in a graceful show.
With humor and joy, they dance away fears,
"Airy elegance! Let's toast with our cheers!"

Lush Green Melodies in Stillness

In cozy corners, they sway with glee,
Whispering secrets of their green jubilee.
Caught in a dance with the sun's shine,
When the dog jumps up, they clear the line!

With soil on the shelf and dust on the floor,
They're plotting a heist for the snack from the drawer.
Potholes of laughter, they giggle and tease,
While the cat eyes them, ready to seize!

When guests come to visit, they put on a show,
With their frilly green skirts, they steal the glow.
Swinging in breezes, playing their part,
Who knew houseplants could rival the heart!

So here's to the greens, the playful display,
In pots filled with tales, they humor the day.
With their leafy levity, sprightly and bright,
They fill our dull hours with laughter and light.

The Guardian Leaves of Home

In the entryway, they stand like knights,
Guarding the home from pesky delights.
With leaves raised high, they laugh at the fuss,
Chasing away dust with leaf-licking thrusts!

Their mission is clear, to protect and amuse,
Warding off boredom, they're never to lose.
When the dog brings in mud, they roll their green eyes,
Who knew plants could also be wise-cracking spies?

They eavesdrop on gossip, they listen with flair,
Sharing smirks with the sunbeams that dare.
The dust bunnies quake, they know what's at stake,
With potting soil power, there's no room for fake!

So here's to the leaves with their quirky charm,
In our home they cheer, spread joy like a balm.
With laughter and light, they keep the gloom away,
Making life's moments a little less gray.

Glimmering Greens and Warmth

In the sunlit spots where they gather to play,
They giggle and wiggle like kids on a day.
Tiny little jungles where mischief abounds,
In a pot, they plot pranks that know no bounds!

With roots like anchors and stems that sway,
They take their stands in a comical way.
Bracing for sunsets and marinating light,
They are the jesters of indoor delight!

Mugs of tea nearby, they know the right time,
To pull off a stunt or a punchline in rhyme.
With laughter in green, they've mastered the game,
Watching us chuckle, they stake their claim!

So here's to those greens, radiant and spry,
Spreading joy in the air, reaching up to the sky.
In pots of pure joy, they're silly and sweet,
Connoisseurs of laughter, they can't be beat.

A Symphony of Leaf and Light

Amidst the sunshine, they shimmy and sway,
Composing a melody bright for the day.
Their leaves like instruments, plucking a tune,
Conducting the chaos in the afternoon!

In a pot, they hold court, a leafy brigade,
With tambourine petals, they boldly invade.
When clumsy feet stumble, they giggle and cheer,
Adding mischief and joy, oh dear, oh dear!

With shadows and sunshine, they spin and they whirl,
Creating a symphony that makes our hearts twirl.
A chorus of green, with a splash of delight,
Filling our days with a laugh in the light!

So here's to the giants that grow by our side,
In leafy adventures, they take us for a ride.
With playful intentions, they dance and they shine,
Creating a melody that's truly divine!

Nature's Soliloquy by the Pane

With leaves all splayed in a leafy dance,
They laugh at dust and take a chance.
Plotting world domination, oh what a scheme,
While I just sip my morning cream.

These greens, so bold, in a pot they sit,
Debating sunshine, they're quite a hit.
They say, 'Who needs a wild forest scene?'
When a cozy windowsill is their dream.

I hear them whisper life's grand debate,
'Who's got the better fate? Us or the plate?'
In sunlight, they strut, quite full of glee,
Dreaming of life as a grand VIP.

But when I water, they just complain,
'Why not a spa, or a shower for gain?'
Yet through it all, their charm's undeniable,
In this leafy drama, they're so reliable.

Verdant Dreams Beyond the Indoor Boundaries

Each morning they stretch in their leafy attire,
Dreaming of jungles, oh to aspire!
With glances at squirrels frolicking free,
'The grass is greener,' they sigh, 'but we're still VIP.'

Poking their heads through the sun-kissed glass,
Planning a trip, oh what a class!
But here they are, in their cozy enclave,
While the stout potted sage seems to rave.

They arch and they sway with a giggle or two,
Making up stories about things they'd do.
'If I were a tree, how grand I'd be,'
But alas, they're just plants, sipping on tea.

In their antics, there's barely a frown,
As they act like royalty donning a crown.
With leaves that are waving like flags in the breeze,
Indoors or out, they thrive with such ease.

The Lush Sanctuary of Home

In the corner, they plot with delight,
While the cat eyes them, ready for a fight.
'The tales we could tell,' I hear them say,
'If only we'd met on a holiday!'

They bounce with joy, soaking up rays,
Discussing their views on gardener's ways.
'Prune me not, or I might get cross!'
'Look at me thriving, you're the real loss!'

Each drip of water brings another retort,
'Is this a garden or a botanical court?'
With sarcasm sharp, they leap with cheer,
Mocking my worries, oh, how they steer!

Yet, through all the chatter and leafy banter,
They remind me of nature's quirky canter.
In a world of pots, they shine ever bright,
Turning my home into a comedy site.

Whispered Secrets in Shades of Green

Nestled in pots, they plot and they scheme,
Whispering secrets like a verdant dream.
'Grow taller!' cries one with a leafy shout,
'I'll show you how to stand tall, without a doubt!'

In the tranquil corner of my sunny space,
They trade crinkle-crackle notes with grace.
'If only we could escape this mundane fate,'
They whisper of adventures, it's never too late.

With a swish and a sway, they cut up and tease,
'A new leaf today, I'll do as I please!'
They parse sunlight like gossip in cafes,
Raising spirits through their leafy ballet.

Homebound heroes in a green costume parade,
Creating a wonderland, sharp wit displayed.
They laugh, they chime, in an indoor spree,
With each whispered secret, they jest just for me.

Sunbeams Through a Green Canopy

A chorus of leaves, they wiggle and sway,
Dancing to tunes that the sunlight will play.
They gossip with dust motes, a twist and a twirl,
Whispering secrets in a shy leafy swirl.

Laughter erupts from the soil below,
As roots tell the story of things that they grow.
A sprout jokes with shadows, it's all in good fun,
While petals debate who gets kissed by the sun.

Each morning they stretch, a comedic routine,
Pretending to yawn, oh what a scene!
The laughter of nature, a very green art,
With a wink and a nod, they play their part.

When evening wraps all in a cozy embrace,
The leaves tell their tales with a leafy grace.
They know they're the stars, with their curls and their flair,
In the sunbeam's spotlight, with nary a care.

A Breath of Earth in the Room

In the corner, they sit, all spunky and spry,
With a flair for the funny, they reach for the sky.
They poke out their fronds, a cheeky charade,
Making the sunlight feel slightly delayed.

With roots that are tickled by whimsical dreams,
They snicker and giggle in pitter-patter schemes.
They serenade air with a soft, leafy joke,
As dust bunnies dance, in a blissful yolk.

Each morning, they cheer for the postman, it seems,
Who delivers the mail of their fanciful dreams.
They plot minor mischief undeterred by the broom,
While charming the air in their earth-scented room.

At night, they host parties, unfurling their fronds,
Communing with shadows and fairy-tale wands.
Joy echoes softly, a playful abode,
In laughter and light, their green kingdom flowed.

Window Sills and Evergreen Tales

On the sill, they gather, a merry brigade,
Plotting grand tales in the dappled shade.
Each leaf's a storyteller with quirks and with charms,
Telling tall tales of their leafy alarms.

One sprout dared to whisper, 'I'm taller than you!'
While others chimed in, 'Well that's nothing new!'
With wriggles and giggles, the laughter ran deep,
As sunlight peeked in, interrupting their sleep.

"Look at us shine!" one said with a grin,
"While the outside world rushes, we just spin!"
They chuckled together, a brotherly crew,
Holding court on the sill like a leafy debut.

In the cloak of twilight, they sigh and unwind,
Sharing their stories, so witty and kind.
As stars twinkle bright in the velvet-like sky,
They bask in the warmth of their quilted reply.

The Hidden Life of Indoor Flora

Inside the walls, a circus unfolds,
With antics and giggles that never grow old.
Each tendril a jester, each leaf a delight,
Putting on shows that last into the night.

In whispers they speak, the sound of a breeze,
With puns about soil and teasing the bees.
They trade silly secrets while catching the light,
As shadows play tag in the softness of night.

A pot stands in wait, for its time to shine,
While roots make the rounds, with a glass of fine wine.
They're savvy and clever, these sprites of the soil,
Chasing laughter like rabbits, as love starts to coil.

Underneath it all, there's joy in the green,
With creatures unseen cradling their scene.
So here's to the hidden, the jokes that they weave,
In the cozy world where all green things believe.

Secrets of the Sunlit Leaves

Sunlight spills through quirky panes,
A dance of shadows, silly gains.
Leaves wiggle, giggle in the light,
Whispering secrets, oh what a sight!

A spider tries to spin a web,
But ends up tangled; what a ebb.
Laughter hides in every fold,
The stories of green, continually told!

A raindrop slips, the drains are near,
Plants chuckle softly, can't show fear.
Grown tall and proud, with a cheeky smirk,
They think they own this windowed perk!

Each leaf's a wink, a silent joke,
Complaints of droppings, the gardener's poke.
Swap positions, just for fun,
Nature's jesters, second to none!

Sheltered Dreams in Leafy Lattice

In the cozy corners, a leafy crew,
Plotting adventures, what shall they do?
With pots for thrones and dirt for couches,
They dream of the day when the sun sur-repouches!

Whispers of mischief, oh how they'd play,
Racing the shadows and sun's golden ray.
One leaf declares, "I'm a star today!"
The others roll over, in green dismay!

A tiny bug sneaks in for a ride,
"Hold on tight!" yells the fussy pride.
The leaves hold a party, just one more day,
For a laugh-filled breeze in the sunny bay!

Dancing to Bach from the dusty shelf,
They slide and twirl, oh what a self!
Bound by laughter, not by the pot,
In this leafy lattice, they find their lot!

Nature's Curtain of Green

A verdant curtain sways and sings,
As Elf and Pixie play with springs.
Bouncing light dances with glee,
The plants exchange a secret spree!

"Look out there!" one leaf exclaims,
"It's a squirrel wearing silly names!"
Foliage chuckles, sways with delight,
Mischiefs abound in the warm sunlight!

Pests come knocking, but who will care?
The leaves just laugh at the commotion there.
They've hatched a plan for a masquerade,
In the heart of green, friendships made.

Through the window, the world peeks in,
A gathering of green where jokes begin.
Nature revels in laughter's flight,
While the curtain of green blocks out the night!

The Quiet Dance of Houseplants

Houseplants gather with a secretive sway,
In the light of the morn, they giggle away.
Quietly shuffling, they practice their moves,
Under the radar, in their leafy grooves.

One little sprout thinks it's quite a pro,
While others snicker, "Oh, look at that show!"
They twirl and they spin, all in a hush,
Mocking the sunlight's warm, gentle rush.

"Step to the left, then back to the right!"
A plant calls out in the flickering light.
They toss their fronds with youthful flair,
Creating a dance not a soul would dare!

With tiny pots, they're kings of the floor,
Each twist and each turn, they can't help but roar.
In their own little world, they sway and they prance,
The quiet brigade, in a leafy romance!

A Dance of Delicate Fronds

In corners green, they spin and sway,
As if they've planned a leafy ballet.
Their tiny stems twist with delight,
In the soft glow of morning light.

One slips and slides across the floor,
Pretending it's in a grand encore.
A tap dance here, a shimmy there,
Who knew plants could have such flair?

They chatter through the gentle breeze,
Gossiping like old friends with ease.
Casting shadows that bounce and play,
They glow in the sun, come what may.

With cheeky smiles and playful grins,
These little leaves know where joy begins.
In every rustle and soft sigh,
They've got a party—oh my, oh my!

The Enchanted Indoor Garden

In pots they sit, a merry lot,
Plotting escapes in a verdant plot.
With tiny boots and silly hats,
They giggle with the curious cats.

A chard rogue tried to hitch a ride,
On a tiny beetle as their guide.
Through windows wide they'd frolic and leap,
With pranks that make the neighbors peep.

When the sun comes shining through,
They flex and stretch, a leafy crew.
No lawn to dance, but oh, what cheer!
Each leaf has a mantra to persevere.

So here's to greenery full of glee,
Chasing away all gloom, you see.
With whimsy and joy wrapped all around,
In this indoor realm, laughter abounds!

Where Nature Meets the Hearth

Nestled near the glowing flame,
These greens all play a leafy game.
With every crackle, they jump high,
Awkward twirls, oh my, oh my!

One leans close, gets too much heat,
Says, "I'm baking! Isn't this sweet?"
But in the corner, potting soil,
Is where their humor truly roils.

They tease the kettle, play tag with steam,
Imagining they're in a giant dream.
Each leaf a comedian, with stellar wit,
Joking 'bout photosynthesis and how to sit.

Even the dust bunnies join the fun,
As botanical merriment is never done.
Around the fire, warmth they bring,
In this quirky home, laughter takes wing!

Tranquil Greens in Morning Light

At dawn, they stretch with yawns galore,
Looking ready for a brand-new lore.
They whisper jokes to tickle the mind,
In this calm space, a joy to find.

Sipping dew like morning tea,
With tiny cups of glee, you see.
Each leaf a jester, dancing bright,
Making mundane mornings feel just right.

Upon the sill, they shake and sway,
Inviting silliness to stay.
Who knew tranquility could be so loud?
These green pals sure make their folks proud!

So raise a glass of sunlight's gleam,
To happy fronds and nature's dream.
With laughter woven in verdant threads,
Joy sprouts here as the humor spreads!

Living Decor: A Touch of Nature

Leaves dance with glee, swaying near the light,
Dust bunnies gather, thinking it's quite a sight.
Pots look like hats, perched up tall and proud,
Do plants gossip softly when the sun's not loud?

Watering can grins like a silly old fool,
Dirt on the table, but I'll play it cool.
Cacti come close, sharing laughs in the shade,
Do they roll their eyes when my scheme's been weighed?

The spider plant hangs like it's taking a dip,
I swear it's planning a daring little trip.
The sun plays peekaboo, and we all join in,
My leafy pals know how to make me grin!

But when I forget, oh dear, what a mess,
They droop, they pout, in leafy distress.

Growth Chronicles in Quiet Spaces

Chlorophyll party? Oh yes, it's true!
They dress up in green, just to match with you.
Tails of the spider plant waving hello,
While the pot asks, 'Is that a new glow?'

Succulents on shelves are plotting their route,
To find the means to stage a little shootout.
But in a quiet stretch, they play it just right,
Claiming my snacks, but they're on a strict diet!

With daylight savings, they play hide and seek,
Peeking through curtains, oh how they squeak!
They giggle at shadows, their playful charade,
Embracing the light in this bright masquerade.

As I water them gently, they cheer with delight,
"More, please! We love the splash and the light!"
Maybe next week, I'll host a grand bloom,
Invite all the pots for a leafy costume!

Nature's Resilience Through Panes

Through glassy escape routes, they plot and they scheme,
How to reach the outdoors, a most glorious dream.
Sun rays are agents, and they help in the quest,
"Join us for brunch," invites the sun's warm zest!

Under the table, they whisper and joke,
"Did you hear about Gary? The caught-in-a-smoke?"
Last week he got crispy, thought he could toast,
Now he's just a relic; they giggle and boast.

With new leaves emerging, they flaunt their fresh show,
The pride of the plant world, they just overflow.
And when I forget them? Oh, the scandalous fate,
With eyes wide and drooping, they act like my date!

Yet through all mishaps, they stick with the game,
Knock-knock jokes between the roots, oh how they claim!

Growing together in this cozy space,
Joking on the sidelines, life's a leafy race!

Whispers of the Green Guardians

In the cozy corner, they wiggle and sway,
Guardians of giggles, they lighten the day.
Their whispers are secrets, whispered soft and sweet,
Every little stir, it's a dance on repeat!

A cheeky little fern plays a prank on the cat,
"Hey, whiskers, come closer, just for a chat!"
But fluffball retreats, and he swishes his tail,
"Those leafy green guards? They're chasing my trail!"

Cacti hold meetings at the edge of the pot,
Sharing tales of adventures, and secrets they've caught.
Rolling their spines in mischievous jest,
"Careful, dear soil, who's joining our fest?"

Tropical dreams bloom in this house so neat,
Mischief afoot, they won't face defeat.
Come rain or shine, they throw leafy raves,
Nature's own wonders, forever so brave!

Enigmatic Green Cradles

In corners they sway with grace,
Like dancers in a silent place.
Tales of jungle, whispers low,
In messy pots where they dare to grow.

A leaf once found a comfy chair,
And claimed it as its throne right there.
A dusty window's cozy scene,
Where sunlight wakes the mischievous green.

Touched by Nature's Finesse

A curious sprout with a comic twist,
Waving hello on nature's list.
But what it wanted most, you see,
Was just a big cup of chamomile tea!

Lush greens that giggle as they drink,
While plotting escapes in sunlight's wink.
Every pot a hearty laugh,
A happy race to soak and gaff!

A Canvas of Leaves and Light

In a world where sunlight plays,
Leaves throw shadows, a leafy ballet.
A game of hide and seek all day,
While dust bunnies start to sway!

With sprinkles of earth on every leaf,
They giggle in whispers, quite the relief.
A sunbeam stretches for its snack,
While leafy friends stage a comical act!

Nurtured Life in Light's Embrace

A cheerful green in a sunlit show,
Wearing dirt like a badge, don't you know?
They wave tiny fronds in delight,
In a playful sway from morning to night.

Shadows dance under the quirky leaves,
Where mischief brews, and laughter weaves.
With a flick and a twist, they sing their tune,
Life's a giggle under the moon!

Reflections of Growth Against Clear Walls

In the corner, they stretch and sway,
Dancing lightly, come what may.
Each frond a wig, in sunlight's gleam,
They plot grand schemes, or so it seems.

Invisible friends with leafy plans,
Conspiring quietly, holding hands.
No need for snacks, they fill the space,
With whispers soft, like a warm embrace.

They peek at folks, with curious glee,
What will you share? A mystery!
No chatter here, just rustling cheer,
In a leafy world, we've nothing to fear.

With every twist, they laugh aloud,
A cheeky clan, forever proud.
They're living large, in pots of clay,
Who knew plants could be so sassy today?

Whispering Green Hearts in Sunlight

A shy little leaf waves to a fly,
"Buzz on over, don't be shy!"
The sunbeams giggle, give them a whirl,
As tiny boots tap, giving twirls.

Little bugs seat in leafy chairs,
Exchanging secrets, without any cares.
"Why don't we grow a party tonight?"
"Just don't forget the snacks that must bite!"

Laughter erupts with a gentle rustle,
As plants proclaim: "We are not just muscle!"
Funny little greenery, plotting and thieving,
Their jokes sprout wings, always believing.

Sun-dropped dreams twinkle up high,
With playful shadows that leap and fly.
In this nook, joy cannot hide,
For every leafy heart feels so alive!

The Poetry of Leaves and Light

Words escape, in green delight,
As leaves compose a silly sight.
They write their tales with sunbeam pens,
In a world where laughter never ends.

"Once upon a time," a sprout began,
"Tiny plants became a fan!"
The vines entwined with dreams so bright,
Shining bold in the soft moonlight.

Each little twist, a line to tell,
Of mischief grown in their leafy swell.
They jest and dance, a leafy din,
Inviting all to join their spin.

So raise a glass to these green bards,
Who spin their yarns in joyous yards.
With laughter sealed in each small vein,
It's a verdant world, where more is gained!

Soothing Shades of Emerald

A couch of green with a soft embrace,
Whispers of humor float all over the place.
One leaf yawns wide in the afternoon glow,
And says, "I'm just here, taking it slow!"

Two sprigs chat with a giggling flair,
"Did you hear the one about the garden chair?"
As sunlight dances, they share with glee,
"Let's throw the best show, just you and me!"

In this tiny jungle, the laughter swells,
From clumsy ants to the blushing shells.
Each day's a canvas for silly art,
Where emerald shades heal every heart.

So come close, friends, to this leafy crowd,
Where giggles grow, and are always loud.
In every corner, life's absurd play,
Creates a dance that brightens the day!

www.ingramcontent.com/pod-product-compliance
Lightning Source LLC
Chambersburg PA
CBHW071127130526
44590CB00056B/2835